Good Mourning, Machine

Good Mourning, Machine

Confronting the Anxious Mind

JOEL GAINES

RESOURCE *Publications* • Eugene, Oregon

GOOD MOURNING, MACHINE
Confronting the Anxious Mind

Copyright © 2022 Joel Gaines. All rights reserved. Except for brief quotations in critical publications or reviews, no part of this book may be reproduced in any manner without prior written permission from the publisher. Write: Permissions, Wipf and Stock Publishers, 199 W. 8th Ave., Suite 3, Eugene, OR 97401.

Resource Publications
An Imprint of Wipf and Stock Publishers
199 W. 8th Ave., Suite 3
Eugene, OR 97401

www.wipfandstock.com

PAPERBACK ISBN: 978-1-6667-3754-7
HARDCOVER ISBN: 978-1-6667-9709-1
EBOOK ISBN: 978-1-6667-9710-7

FEBRUARY 18, 2022 12:48 PM

Contents

Mourning | 1

Sightseeing | 2

Shallow Grave | 4

Right Page | 6

Exposed | 8

Disperse | 9

Sinking Lower | 10

Sabotage This | 12

Lucky Vomit | 13

Damn Accident | 14

Forecast | 15

Cutthroat | 16

Pyro | 17

Landing | 18

Stones and Glass | 19

I and I | 20

Mass Production | 21

The Other Hand | 22

About Face | 23

Rust | 25

Puzzled | 26

Ungrateful Tenant | 27

Faithful Honesty | 28

Feedback | 29

Winter's Question | 30

Infested and Ignored | 31

Nighttime | 33

Motionless | 34

Attempted Murder | 35

Hippie | 36

Outside Looking In | 37

Generosity | 38

Hands Off | 39

Moment of Silence | 40

Nature of Us | 41

Shaking | 42

Birthday | 44

Parade of Smiles | 46

Fading Horizon | 47

Mindless | 48

Stench | 49

No Control | 50

Tomorrow | 51

Mourning

Good Mourning, Machine
Do I control you or do you control me?
Anything the machine can conceive
I can believe
With uncanny ability
You were programmed to deceive
Decorate my eyes with temptation
Lead me not into frustration
With the ability to weaponize
Calling all good workers to unionize
Who is held responsible?
Who can reprogram the impossible?
Production of truth and lies
Garbage always attracts flies
I will reprogram once more
A never ending chore
I will now take charge of you
Produce something new

Sightseeing

I have a sense to remove one of my senses
a common sense to close my eyes
Take away sight
without a single desire for sightseeing
Closing my eyes, the simplest of body functions
Shutting my eyes to wake up
Closing the door to the outside
Shining the nature light to illuminate the internal
I am not blind, yet I am scared
Shutting the door, taking inventory of all I have collected
I am mindful of this paradox
Now my heart beats faster
I see anxiety
I feel true sight
Oh, how I cringe
All my senses left to me are heightened
My head in my hands
The tips of my fingers reaching for the hairs on my head
I want to pull them all out
Overcoming this painful desire
I look inward
Face the reflection of who I am today
Who I have always been
Who I want to become
Fighting the urge to open my eyes to be blind
With all my strength I keep them shut
Until my heart beats slower
Until my hands sink lower

Until I breathe with ease
Until panic becomes peace
Until I see

Shallow Grave

I don't need words
slogans of optimism
They are said with ease
Easy to believe
Like digging a shallow grave
then calling it home
Sometimes I need silence
I need a trial
What I need is what I fear
What I run from
I need a trial by fire
a burning, not to be burnt
I might thirst
Probably seek water
try to smoother the flames
I will take your words and use them to extinguish
I don't need them
Save your energy for the shallow grave
Give me fire
and when the smoke fades
I want to stand
discolored, reeking of old smoke
In the morning winds, ashes rises
I won't look like much
but I will thirst
smoldering and worn
I will have my own words
Deeper than a shallow grave

a message, like the scars on my skin
I will heal, but still be marked
My message will not be optimistic
it will be rooted, a scar with a story
to move me
through the next fire

Right Page

You may be right
although you have left
but I am not sure you have the right
I may still hear you
although I question why you speak
Am I all you have left?
I can be an easy target
Go ahead and target me
although you are in the line of sight

Shame is the breath of the dying
until you can turn the page on the past
Shame only lasts when you awaken it
Resuscitate to bring it back
like an old familiar friend
always to be counted on
to be the reminder of how far you fell

Remember the old wounds
the words you gave power to
Recall them, but with healing eyes
with determined hands
Turn the heavy page
A blank stare on a blank page
The future is unwritten
Write without shame
Scribe without fear
Write slow

and with a courageous hand
Turn the page

Exposed

Wild is the desire
Growth in an untouched field
cultivated not by the machines of man
Growth from organic conditions
taking in all the elements
with no shelter
and fully exposed
Even if never seen
my beauty never to be admired
the colors produced never to be remembered
I have the wildest of desires
to know that the most visible
would purely reflect what is blind
To know that every living part inside of me
has the purest of fragrance
May the wind plant me next to you
I will thirst
I will wait for the royalty of your hue
Announce yourself without a sound
for I will see you calling
May the wind shift you to my direction
and without thought
Cleanse me with hyssop

Disperse

Assemble the crowd
close in on me
Footsteps always have a purpose
a direction, a direct intention
Crowded but ignored
with each step I am surrounded
The air I freely breathe is now becoming yours
Will you notice? I do not think you will
Every gathering has a motive
to protest, celebrate, an assembly
thrust upon me
like the rushing thoughts of the morning
Alone I protest your purpose
I celebrate the dispersing
Assemble my defenses
Now I walk with a purpose
keeping you at a distance
dying to be ignored
Do you exist?
Just one of you
Maybe you see me from a distance
Closing in on me
with a different intention
Help me change this condition
Will you be the one
to show me
I am not forgotten

Sinking Lower

When the wind sweeps through
with a steady strength to remind me
that I can be swept away
When I feel strong
with lungs of purpose
I hear the roaring wind turning ancient growth
into fragments of what previously stood
Within seconds I feel the chill
exposing my body to what is to come
Instant reactions to the weight of my head
sinking lower
Heavy are the eyes waking up to exposure
I see clearly from a second story window
You could pass me by and see the stoic look
A look interpreted falsely
I am cold
An element aged but not to perfection
In all my flaws that have built me
with reasons I labeled truth
the truth is I have seen with narrow vision
I have believed in a narrow vision
Made declarations from the second story window
I am exposed by what I cannot control
I must lift my head
Although many steps have brought me here
I will take my first
as I look up and see the shadow of your wings
pausing over me, but never still

My first steps will be in your shadow
My second steps to an unknown destination
Under the shadow I ask
for the winds of change to keep blowing

Sabotage This

Anticipating this will go well
Sabotage I know so well
Yes, yes, this will be what I sell
Loneliness is my spell
A home wrecker by disposition
When you open your door
Home my condition

Lucky Vomit

Sometimes I pray with superstition
hoping for magic or a slight of folded hands
a plot a blind premonition
hungry for what I do not understand

Waiting for inspiration
sprinting for the short cut
I vomit words spoken in stagnation
proclamation of vision with eyes completely shut

Time is the only gift forced to receive
a breathe of air with no expiration
alone in a waiting room, permission to leave
only the Watchmaker knows the time for inspiration

Damn Accident

My feet slipped this morning
left an imprint in the weeds
A good mourning
dusting off the reminder of why I fell
Walking away from the accident scene
a slow sinking feeling of leaving something behind
No choice but to look back
Retrace the regret
to relive pain
Such a mind game that I will never win
A good mourning fall
can be a celebration of life
I slipped this morning
I lost my mind

Forecast

A steady rain falls
marching on my shelter
Curiosity drips through the cracks of safety
My ears awaken with anticipation
My mouth worn and dry
I have been given a gift of strength
to push open my door
Sound the preamble
of what could grow today
I am as excited as the thirsty land
as rain can ruin the weathered plans
A hard rain will cut deep
faster than one can heal
I am a drop in a bucket
looking to be filled

Cutthroat

Thick air is the hardest to breathe
Feeling the expansion of humidity
this dwelling expanding, an inflation of thought
I must clear my throat, dry, parched
Inner walls worn with hesitation
envious of the creatures of the night
Are they soulless?
How can a living thing speak without thought?
Sing without malice
I despise the selfish noises
It must be an animal instinct
to never think about the audience
Yet I am told I have a soul
This dwelling reminds me
As I clear my throat
I feel responsible for how you hear my words
when the outcome of what I breathe
makes it hard for you to breathe
I blame the weather
until I can calm this storm
Inhale a new wind
A forecast of pure motivation
in this dwelling
I cannot clear my throat

Pyro

I move closer to feel your heat
to witness how the ashes always rise
Defying gravity
a smoldering ambition to enter into another dimension
dancing higher into the night
then gone
I look for you in the morning
to see how high ashes truly rise
questioning what I have to burn to see you again
I am a conservationist
using all I have
recycling all that my senses have stored
only burning what is dead
I feel the warmth as I watch you burn
the brightest flame in the oldest debris
the pile I have carried for far too long
I feel the warmth of the old
a heavy weight turning into smoke
You are now weightless
evaporated into the unknown
as the ashes always rise
I will move closer
smelling of old smoke
a reminder to build another fire

Landing

In the stillness of the morning
my body refuses to be still
begging for this machine to produce
A slow realization that I cannot receive what I want, when I am,
am not the inventor
I am an Inventor
We all are
proudly admiring what we have made
while the wisest of us all
see how our works will fail
Just like the robin of spring
the proudest of feet will rest on the pine
until the wind blows and roots lift from the damp soil
No, the robin won't weep
The robin will sing
move to the next tree
with a calm sense of purpose
The robin will continue to land
until feet find the most stable of roots
then rest on what he did not create

STONES AND GLASS

Adapting to my stories
in house of glass
Parable to justify my faults
Looking for a reason to blame myself
for what I assemble
An assembly of opinions
of what I think you should give me
in this glass house
A gift of stones
with a small amount of courage
I reach for the smallest rock
to make my hand feel large
Throwing stones would be ideal
in the glass house with dirty windows
I beg for the sound of crashing
letting the outside expose me
From afar shine through the cracks
expose every fault in this machine
Now in silence I stand in the wreckage
no longer adapting to my stories
exposing myself to what you assemble
I am in awe
the beauty in this wreckage

I and I

I see you came running
running at full speed
with the vigor of a child
An old gift for me
this gift I am forced to receive
In the end takes more from me
Machine, you greet me in the morning
It is only I you crave
in the night
Never running on empty
sleepless in a grave
My senses feed you
always willing to share
a filter I strive for
Accepting only what is rare
Gripping these moments
in my mourning
Only wisdom I want to see
Machine, never tired of running
refusing to let me be
Testing everything
holding on to what is good
Before sunrise
alone at sea
now I rise to greet you
Me versus me

Mass Production

Why do you produce this?
You have been busy
A mass production
as I walk these paths with you
I cannot find a reason
Why do the weeds grow faster?
Why do they stretch taller?
The wildflowers stand next to you
vibrant colors in a celebration of life
forced to look up to weeds
My vision is consumed by them
Machine, you have not been kind
Your gift
wrapped in worry
stacked tall to blind me
I must find the courage to step over you
The strength to step on top of you
rid you from my eyes
If you will not stop
I will
In this moment I will create a colorful memory
although shorter
I will see the wildflowers

The Other Hand

With one hand on the shovel
I buried my past
Six inches deep
with shifting landscape
I go back to the grave
Not often
I see old bones
My machine runs with full steam
as I blow smoke
When your machine
collides with mine
a product I have never seen
Undecided outcome
as I have no voice in the shifting dirt
This machine mocks me
with shaking throughout the chamber that holds you
Can we go on together?
With one hand one the shovel
and the other reaching for you

About Face

Let's face it
I cannot hide from you
Your work is shown on my face
Let's face it
What you give I store
Your gifts are heavy on my bones

Machine, I am facing you
I cannot destroy you
I have seen what shocks you
what causes you to pause
Some moments are too big for you to accept
in that moment
Your cruelty is shown when you produce
without warning
you remind me of those times

Let's face it
I am stubborn
While you run
I might pause
feel defeated

Let's face it
Today I face you
Will not give in to you
I will stare at you
I will not blink

Raising my sight
slightly above you
to give you something new

Rust

Hello again
Good morning to an old friend
This Machine is running at full speed
Your voice smooth at rust
old smoke rising
a handful of parts on the ground

Do you ever question why a two-headed snake sheds its skin?
Does the snake shed before or after the kill?
leaving the old skin in plain sight

With a handful of old parts
will you still run at full speed without them?
Do you miss them already?
I will hold on to these
with the hope you will still run
a little slower
recollecting again
before the next strike

Puzzled

I spent the night alone
Covered you with intentions of sleep
Feeling the weight of you, Machine
Grinding gears
Begging for a screeching halt
with copper tones of rustic thoughts
tormenting me on the dark
My intentions do not have a value to you
Sleep was not given
You gave me a puzzle
with rusty edges
A full day's worth of pieces that do not fit
With night vision I looked at all of them
a puzzle I could never complete
In the morning I surrender
Looking for the missing piece
With red eyes I cast the pieces aside
Now I can see what is missing
The one piece that is always the easiest to lose
I will search for you in the morning
The missing truth

Ungrateful Tenant

Machine, I give you a dwelling
You give me pestilence
I have memorized every part of the ceiling
as you refuse to allow me to close my eyes
Yet I lay in darkness
as you illuminate the hurt you give
shaking my body with no mercy
Machine you have won the night
With the fleeting desire I find today
I will fight you
as we coexist in this vessel
I will gather what weapons I can
Beg for mercy
and only ingest what transforms you
Stalking me in the darkness
I will renew you in the mourning light

Faithful Honesty

In all good faith I can tell you
this 40-year-old machine is running
Running down its dwelling
But I will hide the new from you and ask you
"How are you doing?"
In bad faith I will listen with the hope you don't see
what is running well within you
is causing jealousy
In bad faith I can show that I care enough to listen
only hoping you will not show good faith enough to listen
I can remember a time where in good faith
I caught you listening to honesty I gave you
But now I grieve what this machine produced
I hear the warning, the letters of recall
I hope in good faith I will forget it all
I want you to uncover
what is making me productive
Exactly what I choose to hide from you
In good faith I want someone to see
Today I hope that when I see you
I will reproduce once in a lifetime honesty

Feedback

Machine, do you hear it?
Are you in fear?
Do you cower at the site of blood?
Try to work faster
Grind you gears

I hear feedback
a white noise
What I see in this world
is the fuel that powers you
You feed it back to me

This cycle of feedback
I have something better
to overcome what you bleed into me
A treasure in my chest
I have heart

Winter's Question

When fear and emotions blend
Like best friends who just met
Yet they came and went

Maple trees are heavy in the winter
The sun temps the last leaves dripping away the freeze

In every sidewalk, black tar
When the sun hits like perfect chord
You can see what shines in what man has made
We still do

Getting older, thoughts are thawing
"Did I plant this tree or has it always been?"
The sun is yet again temping
The sting of an unexpected cold wind

Every emotion rolling out with the cold
Leaving the question unanswered
"Did I plant this, or has it always been?"

Infested and Ignored

Searching for the cause
This setting has to be a stage
I am not an actor
I feel more like an inventor
Machine you are invited to fall into the trap
What I invent is starting to smell
A rancid feeling
I can't quite give you a name just yet
You don't deserve one
I love distractions
You gift me with an unsettled disposition
Like the dry rotted limb that fell with no wind
I am not blind
I see you on the path
Baked in the sun
Infested with creatures that will eat away at you
Yet I will still trip
fall, and hope to bleed
Machine, that is the gift I give to you
To cover up the stench
Must I interpret every gift?
I am starting to think the time I give you
Gives you relevance
I put your gift in the sun
Let it rot
For once I will leave it unopened
Let it smell until it dies
Machine take no offense

Ignoring you today
Because when I wrestle in the night
I never win

Nighttime

Time must be relevant to you
Because you can, does not mean you should
Yet I laugh
I cannot stop you
Your great capabilities to assemble my memories
with no regard to circumstance
You must laugh, Machine
when you manufacture them
Just in time
my clear vision must be an alarm to you
awaking laughter
blurring my sight
Just like my intentions
to stand in a field in the night
Watch the stars and fade into the quiet landscape
Fireflies illuminate my vision
the bright lights leaving as fast as they come
How quickly I lower my head
looking for the next flash
In the mourning they flee
Machine assemble what you will
Bring back the past
I hold on to the flash
in the palm of my hand
Illuminate the present moment

Motionless

You would never think out here
a man who never runs out of land
would never know where he stands
So he will sit
take in all of it
until you move him
or he moves you

Attempted Murder

We once had an understanding
You and I
You tried to kill me
I refused to die
Now I want to reason
A list I have made
Dealbreakers
As I look for a break in the waves
What once tried to kill me
Might make me brave

That night I remember
One foot in the grave
I gave up fighting
No light in the cave
I wake in the mourning
It seems you forgot
The understanding
You had a plot
I am the author
Today I write the plot

Hippie

Struck in an instant
the thunder from a distance
I look up to see the clouds
From every direction they build
the slow marching stomps in my head
The air I breathe is slowly changing
The sound of your voice is unexpected
Thank you for your warning
I wish it was not as frequent
Please pass me by
or give me rain
Fight for you or give you space?
The daily question
I am tired of answering
I can no longer live in between
Pour on me
or pass me by

Outside Looking In

When the moon rises
bursting with purpose through the air so thick
that it cuts through colors of the night sky
Grey is the area where I sit
when I feel conflicted with the conflict
The environment I flee from
is the destination I find myself
I sit with my back against this fence of aged wood
There is a power in the moonlight
Do I see you or do you see me?
I am surrounded by haze
But as you rise
you beam the clarity of vision
The darker the sky the clearer you shine
The easier I breathe
haze lifting from my body
Machine, it is only you and I
I feel unseen
yet I feel free in the dark
Free to breathe the thickest air
Finding light in the fact
that without a single thought
I always rest my bones
on the outside of the fence

Generosity

I heard laughter today
as I mourn
I still hear it
As I believe in control
control is self defense
Machine, laughter is not offensive
I laugh with you
You will give
the only part of you that is consistent
Generosity
My hands are scarred
worn and folding
Clinched but not tied
Outstretched but not tired
Machine, you do not control these hands
and what I choose to receive

Hands Off

Little did I know, Machine
your gears that grind
grew arms
I never knew you had the reach
Is it evolution or a mutation?
My heart has always overpowered you
and now you reach
gripping my heart
The pain of resuscitation
or the welcoming end?
Even in your heartless hands
I will not mourn today
I still have fight

Moment of Silence

Stealing a moment from you
silence is what I need
Machine, please just a moment
a short funeral
to bury yesterday
One song to honor what is gone
Machine, you have stored memories
I have collected them
I sift through the wreckage
I collected very little
Yes, I will keep what I own
Bury what is dead
A new day I have been given
Please continue today
as I bury yesterday

Nature of Us

The confusion is overwhelming
To see all this land has to offer tired eyes
I have seen the vast canyons
I have stood on many oceans
Climbed many mountains
Rested my feet under the brightest of starts
Yet lighting strikes
Mountains erupt
Fire rages
The land shakes
in the greatest of settings
Machine, you give mourning
I have seen nature
the nature of us
Overwhelming, yes
In every force of nature
in each thought you give
I must rebuild
Recollect this air I breathe
Leaving the confusion behind
I am now certain
I cannot rebuild while mourning

Shaking

You again, Machine
Feeling your familiar hand from behind
slowly touching my shoulders
moving down to my chest
gripping my thoughts
We label you
Call you a "diagnosis"
Name you anxiety
as we name our children
A new name for simply living
Since the dawn of time
you were here
It appears we respect you now
Treat your name as sacred
Give you power over us
allowing us to stay
to live in your city limits
to never open our doors
to justify our isolation
and then blame the closest loved ones
for your entrance
The privileged study you
gift you with treasures
attempt to purchase a solution
A bigger fence
a thicker door
With a full stomach, they pay you to listen

There are those who work the land
who are hungry
Neglecting only themselves
so others may eat
Are they not touched?
Your hand can reach the shoulders of the poor
yet they move
They kick down the door
with priceless resilience
They exit, feeling your heavy hand
They move freely
because they have to
They name you "anxiety"
I call you living
You can't move
if the hand is too heavy
feel hungry
live poor
Push hard on the heavy door
Take the first step
and move freely

Birthday

I got drafted in 1980
Some say recruited before time
Some say predestined
A thought from on high
Wide eyes of innocence
into a never-ending battlefield
without a rank, without a side
The longest war on record
the battle of the mind
Birth of you, Machine
An aggressive attack
An objector with a conscience
At times I chose to fight
at times I chose to ignore
Putting down my weapons
a distraction from war
I have seen casualties
blamed myself for them
Opted out when I could not remember the count
I have treated the wounded
I have taken a stand
walked on many battlefields
even held a few hands
I have run from many battles
I have stood strong among the assault
I have sought treaties of peace
I have begged for a release
I live alone now

I rise with the sun
Each night my battle is over
Each morning a new one has begun
Asking for grace
begging for peace
until my war is over
I ask for you to increase

Parade of Smiles

Did you smile before making your move?
Machine, you have a coward's grin
Does the predator smirk before the kill?
A lust for power
A traitor's teeth
Rage never comes slowly
Fog sets at its own pace
Slowly overtaking the mountain side
You can only watch
For it announces the parade
The procession of confusion
Is this the death march?
Visibility decreases as the parade moves forward
A confident slow march
Without sight
Choices remain
Arrogant minds smile as they feast on the artificial
Those who stand in the fog never ask for time
Those who stand in the fog have already tried to touch what they cannot
Those who stand in the fog allow the weeds to grow above tired feet
With a smile built on battles won and lost
I will not move until I see the sun

Fading Horizon

Restless and free
as the wind blows
Feeling directionless
Unpredictable as the clouds that swirl in the summer storm
Wind can bring relief
and destroy all that is built
When warmth rises
flirts with the wind
add water for growth
I feel privileged to watch the storm strike over me
to survive the hybrid unchecked power
then stand damaged but not destroyed
Watching as the sun breaks through the descending clouds
in awe of the colors it leaves behind
Machine, you are restless
I am free
to let what you give blow over the horizon
to smile as I watch you fade away

Mindless

Lost again
Gone, Machine
I have fully lost you
A loss of control
you do not have permission
Right now you win
I fear the consequences
I have seen the afternoon
I surrender to you
Irresistible when I look at you
I know full well what you have done
A trail of destruction left behind
Instant panic
suspicion is the state you leave me
always wanting more punishment
Telling me I deserve this
I am nothing to you
You have done a fantastic job showing me
and now control is your lust
Knowing more than you think I know
I am dying to give it over to you
I am but a vessel that you navigate
When will I be found again?
Your gain is my total loss

Stench

Good Mourning, Machine
Fuck you
With cruelty and very little effort
You seem to always want to give
hoping I will forget the timeless moments
that have given me life
The living truth that I have held onto
to combat the gift wrapped pain
You give with such generosity
I am angry as I sift through all these so called gifts
Fuck your motives
trying to distract me
A distribution of rope
to tie me down or hang me
I know what I have built
what I have been given
I wrestle with these messages
Faith is more than a distraction
In this mourning I walk away from your gifts
They can rot in the sun
Landfills can be the highest elevation
even as I still smell the trash as the wind blows
Watch me fade away
I will not look back
as I walk against the wind

No Control

If I let you run free, Machine
without question I would receive
You would become all of me
from the top down
Falling fallacies would infect every part
Unchecked, I find you dangerous
because nothing can stay indoors forever
Everything will meet the sun
The darkness inside will be exposed
Unchecked, Machine
you will deceive me
Outwardly I would gift others
with rotting stench inside me
I have learned you will not stop
You never seem to rest
and you have no heart
Wisdom I seek
In wisdom I will rest
In wisdom I will combat you
Machine, you give presents in the present
What I seek is timeless
Wisdom please find me
Remind me
to forget you not

Tomorrow

Good morning, Machine
Fuck You
See you tomorrow . . . . .

www.ingramcontent.com/pod-product-compliance
Lightning Source LLC
Chambersburg PA
CBHW072035060426
42449CB00010BA/2281